The HIDDEN Limp

"Your faith has made you WHOLE."
MATTHEW 9:22

Amy TIMMONS

The HIDDEN Limp

Copyright @ 2021 Amy Timmons
All rights reserved.
ISBN: 979-8-9851725-2-2

Author owns complete rights to this book and may be contracted in regards to distribution. Printed in the United States of America.

Library of Congress Cataloging-in-Publication Data

The copyright laws of the United States of America protect this book. No part of this publication may be reproduced or stored in a retrieval system for commercial gain or profit.

No part of this publication may be stored electronically or otherwise transmitted in any form or by any means (electronic, photocopy, recording) without written permission of the author except as provided by USA copyright law.

Ghostwriting: SynergyEd Consulting/ synergyedconsulting.com
Graphics & Cover Design: Greenlight Creations Graphics Designs

shero publishing

Published by: SHERO Publishing
getpublished@sheropublishing.com
S H E R O P U B L I S H I N G . C O M

The HIDDEN Limp

Amy TIMMONS

The HIDDEN Limp

TABLE OF CONTENTS

Acknowledgments		6
Forward		7
Introduction		8
Chapter One	*Facing My Limp*	12
Chapter Two	*Limp's Paralyzing Progress*	20
Charter Three	*Limp of Fear*	28
Chapter Four	*Limp's Impact on Motherhood*	32
Chapter Five	*Limp of Insecurities*	38
Chapter Six	*Limp's Effect On My Relationships*	44
Chapter Seven	*Limp's Impact on Ministry*	52
Chapter Eight	*Exodus*	58
About the Author		70

Acknowledgments

I want to send a special thank you to everyone who believed in me and in this project. That list includes (but is certainly not limited to):

My children, Joseph and Joshua Clayton
My grandchildren, Lauryn and Kamryn Clayton, and Javian Fauntleroy
My parents, Henry Timmons, Jr. and the late Gloria Timmons
My sister and my brothers
My family (sisters-in-law, nieces, nephews)
The members of Awakening Outreach Church, Inc
Mrs. Ann Miles, my doula
Ms. Marva Matthews
Mrs. Joan King

Foreword

*"It took a long, long road to get here.
It took a brave, brave girl to try..."*
-Alicia Keys

Resilience is an admirable trait that speaks to one's possession of both grit and grace. It is an ongoing process of being reset and reformed that is, in its truest sense, lifelong. Like the sea, it has its ebbs and flows, with each movement bringing and carrying lessons that we need to learn. ***The Hidden Limp*** by Amy Timmons precisely captures her journey of becoming that gives her readers access to the recesses of her soul. It is a written embodiment of both wounds and wonders that chronicle her endurance of a transformative evolution from people-pleasing and fear, to launching out into the deep with divinely-inspired fortitude and courage.

Paulleatha Bruce, MDiv

Introduction

"Are not two sparrows sold for a penny? Yet not one of them will fall to the ground outside your Father's care."
Matthew 10:29 (NIV)

I never felt confident enough to share my life openly with anyone. This is my survival narrative, aimed at those like myself who allowed their lives to be defined by the things that happened. A story only I can tell. This is my attempt at revealing the excellency of our God. He can take the messes of our life and make exceptional stories and orchestrate great victories. Now, I realize everything that happened in my life was preparation, and my Father was aware of it all. That is why it is so important for me to share with you my journey, "Through many dangers, toils, and snares I have already come; 'tis grace has brought me safe thus far, and grace will lead me home." This book means a lot to me because it is a journey of self-discovery, survival, heartache, forgiveness, and healing. I heard someone say, "appearance is everything," they forgot to mention how exhausting it is to keep up appearances. For years from the outside, I appeared to have it all together. On the inside, I have been limping through life, and to be frankly honest, I am exhausted. I want to share this journey with the hope that you will find freedom and healing from your limp. Pain is all-inclusive; doesn't discriminate, male or female, nor does it matter your ethnicity or your economic level.

What is a limp? Webster defines a limp as a gait impeded by injury or stiffness. Nelson's Illustrated Dictionary defines *lame* as "a disability in one or more limbs, especially in a foot or leg, so that person experiences difficulty in walking or moving freely." There are limps that are visible to the naked eye, and there are limps, like mine, that are hidden from sight. Those hidden limps come in the form of insecurity, shame, lack of discipline, fear, and a need to please others. By exposing and addressing the limp in our lives, we will be able to take ownership of the limp and begin the healing process. The first step to my healing was admitting I was in pain. It was important to me to take ownership of my limp so that I could decide how, when, or even if my limp affects my life. *Webster's Dictionary* defines t*rauma* "as a deeply distressing or disturbing experience." Most limps are caused by some type of trauma in one form or another -- disappointments, molestation, divorce, and dysfunction. It doesn't matter whether visible or invisible the limp has the same effect. It impedes freedom of movement.

There will be people in your life who will recognize your limp, your weakness and use it as a form of control and manipulation. There will be those who recognize your limp and will be satisfied to allow you to remain impeded because it allows them to appear larger than they are. Then there will be those in your life willing to walk alongside you to strengthen and encourage you. Your role is to recognize the difference, know the people in your circle and be willing to expose the frauds. It takes discernment to distinguish between them. Here is where our trust in God is important because He alone knows the heart of a person. In my woundedness, there were times I was unable to determine who was for me and who was against me.

Revelation: Everyone can't go where you are going. And everyone doesn't want to see you succeed.

I have allowed my limp to limit my life and relationships, both personally and professionally. With every encounter with God, He has reminded me there are no limits in Him. The only limits in my life and in your life are the limits we impose on ourselves. Stop seeing the glass as half empty and begin to see it as half full. The world is yours to have.

Freedom is what you and I have been striving for, freedom to love, be loved, and to obtain our goals. Often our failure to reach and secure them can be traced to a "limp" in an area in our life that causes us to falter along the way. We have been identifying with the wrong thing. We must begin to identify with success in every area of our lives. Life's limitations aren't always physical, a missed place word, a broken heart, verbal abuse, and rejection. You and I aren't bound to a mat, yet we have been bound and limited by childhood trauma and other outside forces most times beyond our control. Today God wants to set you free. This journey we are about to undertake will change your life just as it has changed mine. Together, let's walk out into our potential. This book is your marching orders. Like any true commander, I am giving you a command to "RISE UP!" RISE UP and declare I am more than this. I look forward to walking alongside you as together we move from limited to unlimited. Thank you for taking the journey with me. We will change our view. I hope you know life looks different from the penthouse...

Please pray with me. Father God, we humbly submit ourselves to you. Father, we admit today we have allowed our lives to be hijacked by pain, trauma, and abuse, and in so doing, we have limited Your ability to work in our lives. Without You taking this journey with us, we are powerless to overcome. We acknowledge our weaknesses. We need You. Today we surrender the trauma, the heartache, and those that perpetrated the trauma to your care. Help us to walk in forgiveness as You have forgiven us. We commit the rest of our lives to You, and it begins today. Thank you, Father, for guiding us to this moment. Open our hearts to receive the words in these pages, give us strength to embrace the leading of the Holy Ghost, who empowers. In Your hands, AMEN
I am ready for change, and it begins with You. It begins today.

Let us begin......

The HIDDEN Limp

Amy TIMMONS

Chapter 1:
Facing the Limp

"And we know that all things work together for good to them that love God, to them who are the called according to his purpose." Romans 8:28 (KJV)

"Life, for me ain't been no crystal stair. It's had tacks in it, and splinters and boards torn up, And places with no carpet on the floor, bare."[1]

Through it all, I learned how to smile. Unfortunately, a trait I learned, I wanted to say, inherited. However, unhealthy habits are learned behavior, not inherited behavior. I have smiled and laughed my way through life only to arrive here, at a place where I realize my smiles were fake. My laughter was filled with disappointment, hurt, and failure. No, my life hasn't been easy. I truly believe that everything that has happened in my life will eventually work for me and no longer be against me. There are some things that happened in my life that were meant to and probably should have killed me, but God. There are choices I made in my life that I knew were wrong, and I still chose to do it. Not only did people hurt me, but I also hurt myself. However, I have learned that if we place it in God's hand, He can make diamonds out of our coal. In the book of Acts, we meet a man lame from birth, his life as he knew it was normal, and he never dreamed it could be different, so he naturally

---

[1] Langston Hughes, Mother to Son.
https://www.poetryfoundation.org/poems/47559/mother-to-son

settled in and became comfortable. How many of us have stopped dreaming and have accepted the life we were given as normal? We believe the abuse is normal, the dysfunction is normal, and the hatred is normal? Well, it is not normal. In God's kingdom, He can use the abnormal to change our lives. God can turn failure, disappointment, heartache, and pain where it will work for your benefit, turn your lemons into lemonade. I have often felt the pain of my limp, and until now, I never knew the steps to get my healing.

It wasn't one thing I could point my finger at that caused me to feel the way I felt or to react the way I did. I believe it was a series of events, a dysfunctional family dynamic, molestation, being bullied, being rejected by my peers, deep insecurity, a need to please others, and fear. All contributed to my limp. I entrusted my life to people who declared their love for me, only to be left disappointed, broken, and confused. I had to recognize some of the events which led to my limp were out of my control, and I no longer needed to accept the belief *"it was somehow my fault."* My life was changed because people didn't consider my feelings nor the impact their actions would have on my life. The bully that saw what they perceived as a weakness to be exploited created havoc on my self-esteem. It was their decision to molest me, to have an affair, to lie, to leave, and to reject me. The bullies who saw what they perceived as a weakness to be exploited, created havoc on my self-esteem. It was their decision. The impact of the decision of others, on my life, have been far-reaching; effecting my every decision or lack thereof.

Trauma produces a ripple effect. It is like throwing a pebble in the lake. The displacement of the water creates this ripple which extends out from the initial splash. Likewise, trauma can create the same effect in a person's life. My experiences sent ripples throughout my life, ripples of low self-esteem, fear, and the need to please people. These ripples have in some way or another affected my entire life, my relationships, ministry, parenting, and my dreams. I often prayed for the molestation to end. However, when it did, my reaction was the opposite of what one would expect. Yes, I felt a sense of relief. Yet, there were times that I wondered what was wrong with me. *Am I not good enough?* A child associates attention with love, and if there is no or minimal attention, a child feels unloved or assumes something is wrong with them. In my cry for freedom, I became confused, and instead of being excited that my abuse had ended, and I could move on, I wondered *why* it stopped. This experience left me trying to figure out what I had done to cause it and to make it stop. I think initially, I thought it was a game that went horribly wrong. I genuinely believe this was when I developed the need to please people. *If I do everything they ask or do everything right, they won't leave.* My self-worth was crippled, my viewpoint was distorted, and with it came a whole lot of shame because I felt the way I did. This created a vacuum that I wanted so desperately to fill, and it didn't matter with what I filled it: bad relationships, poor choices, or self-doubt. I never knew how far-reaching those moments would ripple in my life. I left the experience and went about life as if nothing ever happened, unaware of the real consequence of the trauma.

I don't remember the exact day; I just remember thinking I wasn't good enough and applying that thought to my life. Have you ever believed and applied your toxic thoughts to your life? I had no concept of affirming myself or how to implement affirmations in my life. Affirmation may have been the means for me to win the fight that was raging in my mind. I accepted every thought as factual and never considered weighing it again what God has always said about me. I fell into the trap of giving every thought precedence over the matchless voice of God. And no matter what I did, expensive clothes, nice shoes, or luxury items, inside, I still wasn't good enough. I allowed the voice of my limp to drown out the voice of God.

Revelation: Don't beat yourself up. The good news is there is a Way out.

I shared in *"Our Stories His Glories,"* a book compilation that I had the privilege of being a co-author, that I was hiding *"In Plain Sight."* I was hiding my limp from the world around me. And some of you have been doing the same thing. Very few people in my life knew the real me. Who was I hiding from, the world or myself? At the root of my limp was sin; either the sin of others or my own, and the result of the sin is guilt and shame. The lie that shame wants you to believe is no one cares, and no one will understand. Well, I understand. I understand the guilt of lying to yourself, the shame of being a victim, and the shame of the choices you made. I get it, and so does God. Shame is defined in *Webster's Dictionary* as "a painful feeling of humiliation or distress caused by the consciousness of wrong or foolish behavior." I allowed shame to push me in the closet, and to be honest, I was content to be in there until it got overcrowded with regret. A life of regret is no life at all. It is time for me, and it is time for you to live. I realized it was impossible for me to reveal the real me when I spent the majority of my life trying to be someone else, someone perfect. Impossible.

Revelation: You must be careful what you allow in your life. Everything and everyone isn't meant for you.

When my mother was dying, I wrote in my journal, "*What is behind the laughter?*" My mom had a quick wit; she would make you laugh until your side hurt. All the while, she would keep this stoic look on her face. I love those memories. While sitting there beside her bed, I wondered, was her laughter her way of hiding her pain? I will never know. I tried to hide from the world. It is easier to hide than to explain.

My limp has been my constant companion, like a guest that won't leave. You may think what happened in your life hasn't affected you. I beg to differ. Looking back, my limp has in some way affected every relationship or lack of a relationship in my life. The man in the book of Acts who lay at the Beautiful Gate, suffered from lameness since birth. His condition affected every aspect of his life, from his ability to provide financially for himself, his dependence on others, and his ability to worship God. Today I own my limp because, in some way, it has shaped who I am, and therefore it will always be a part of me. Now I can determine how or if it will affect my future. I am taking back my control. Because of my limp, I never figured out who I could be. I kept people at a distance, never allowing them to see the real me, afraid they would reject me. NOW, I am ready to show the world who I am.

A friend asked me to go for a ride, our families were acquainted with each other for years. He was my first crush. We had lost touch with each other for many years, and when he returned and showed up at my door, I was excited to see him. I hopped at the opportunity to take that ride with my friend from the past. You never think things will happen to you. I thought it was a chance for us to get caught up. It was a short ride to our destination. Along the way, we laughed and talked about everything we had been doing during our years apart. Both of us had changed. We ended up at what I presumed to be his parents' home. We entered a building, "a man cave," it had all the cliché items a bar, stereo system, TV, and a couch. We sat on the couch, continued to talk, and reminiscence about days gone by. The situation organically shifted to us kissing and *making out*, and it went further than I was ready for. I asked him to stop. He did not heed my request, and I said again, "Stop!" He refused to stop, and it resulted in me forcefully pushing him away. He got up and said, "Come on, let me take you home." The mild-mannered person I had known, changed to this cold, distant person. We drove back in silence. The drive there had been short, but the drive home was long. We arrived at the "circle" of the cul-de-sac, he stopped the car and said, "Get out." There was no goodbye, no laughter, no "good to see you." He wasn't the boy that left all those years before, he was demanding from me what I wasn't ready to give, it wasn't the same. This incident further ingrained in me- *just do what people want, they will like you, accept you, and they won't leave you.* I could handle doing whatever people wanted. What I couldn't handle was the rejection. I "limped" back up the hill to my house, sure of one thing, I was broken. I was broken because a relationship I once cherished and trusted was now the source of a new wound. If I couldn't trust him, who could I trust?

Many years later, my theory of "people-pleasing" was proven wrong. A person I loved with my whole heart started hearing noises outside of the house at night, and because I did not hear the noises, I was told I was lying, and I was hiding something. True to form, to pacify him, I agreed someone, indeed, was outside the house. This man that I loved, told me that the person outside the house was there because of me; that I was having an affair! I was naïve enough to believe time would reveal the truth. It never happened. I was never able to convince them it wasn't true. The relationship still ended. Years after the fact, we were in an intense argument over something unrelated and he brought up the subject of the affair again. He still held on to the belief I had an affair. Damned if I do and damned if I don't! At the end of the relationship, I was broken, lost, and clueless to who I was, and who I could trust. What happens when in your best effort, it still isn't good enough? I wasted so much time trying to be what everyone else wanted me to be, and to make sure everyone else was happy, I lost myself in the process. I had to learn to be true to myself because pleasing people didn't guarantee me love or happiness. It only led to me sacrificing bits of myself, my needs, my dreams, and my faith in myself, all to accommodate someone else's weaknesses.

There was an occasion when I was in a store, and there was a pair of shoes on sale for ten dollars. I had the means to purchase the shoes. However, I had spent so much time taking care of others and allowing others to make decisions for me, that I couldn't even make a decision to buy the shoes. I did eventually buy the shoes after I walked outside, sat in my car, and talked to myself for a while, a loooooong while. I am sure the people in the store thought something was seriously wrong with me when in truth, I had difficulty making decisions. That day was monumental for me. For once in my life, I chose myself, and I regained my ability to make decisions for myself. It was so simple, yet so difficult.

Revelation: Never sacrifice yourself for someone else. If they love you, they won't want you to. They will help to enhance you.

Chapter 2:
Limp's Paralyzing Progress

"...but your master's grandson Mephibosheth shall always eat at my table."
2 Samuel 9:10

In order to achieve anything in this life, it is going to require a decision and movement on your part. Any movement is better than not moving at all. There were times in my life when I was moving forward only to come to an abrupt halt or take a couple of steps back. I struggled to reach the goals and plateaus I set for myself. I realize my "limp" kept me from moving professionally, spiritually, and emotionally. *Webster's Dictionary* defines *limp* as "impeding forward progression." Sometimes I have felt like that nine-year-old girl all over again, waiting for someone to approve or give me permission to be great. The best way to describe it is, as a *time warp*. I am much older now, and yet there have been times in my life when I was still waiting and hoping for someone to affirm me. Social media has us all looking for likes. We must believe in ourselves, even with or without the likes. What I have learned is if you don't believe in yourself, it is virtually impossible to believe you will be successful at anything. What we say about ourselves should line up with what God is saying about us. I am guilty of believing what everyone else was the "gospel." I faltered in life when I failed to believe I "am fearfully and wonderfully made," and when I failed at that, I struggled to believe other things God had said about me.

Revelation: God's very character is truth and love. He can't lie. If He said it, then it shall come to pass. You and I can take that to the bank, it is good.

Instead of believing the voice of God, I wasted time waiting on others to approve of me when the only one that mattered was God.

Revelation: The one you are looking to approve of you is struggling with their own identity.

I would see everyone else succeeding, doing what they were destined to do unafraid, unhindered, and unashamed, and I envied them. I often asked myself, "What in the hell is wrong with you?" People weren't keeping me from sitting at the table. I was keeping myself from the table. The only difference between others and me is they possessed something I lacked, belief in their ability to perform the task before them and a willingness to do it afraid. I was sick of the hamster wheel never moving forward, always just going around and around. Yet, I had no idea how to get off until now. The *spiraling* is like the gravitational pull of the earth. When you fall, you want to stop, but the pull is too great, and all you can do is brace yourself for impact and try to prevent getting hurt, but you still fall. The question was asked, "Why does the hamster keep going around on the little wheel?" The answer is because he has no choice. He is dependent on someone else to take him off the wheel. Unlike the hamster, you and

I have a choice, and I choose ME. If I dare ask, what has you stuck on the wheel? Freedom is at your fingertips. It is as close as the words in your mouth, SPEAK, freedom is yours. As for me, I am no longer making decisions based on fear, rejection, low self-esteem, and the need to please people, because when I did, the outcome was not always pretty.

One incident in particular, stands out among many. When I was seventeen, at the start of my life, I wanted so desperately to go to the University of North Carolina at Chapel Hill. One summer, I was given the opportunity to spend a couple of days on campus at College Experience Camp with several of my classmates. The days on campus passed quickly, but we made a lot of memories. I was in love with the campus and with the idea of being on my own, all of it. But when it came time to apply, my insecurities kicked in, and I was unwilling to leave home. The voices in my head kept me paralyzed. *You won't be accepted, you are not smart enough, you aren't good enough!* This was that same demoralizing voice that I accepted as my truth. I had the grades, the SAT scores, and my parents were on board. There was nothing stopping me or was there? I had the necessary tools to succeed; I was just not equipped to use them. I allowed my insecurities to take my dream from me. I was the hamster on the wheel. So, I got a job and went to community college. My insecurities followed me. I enrolled in computer science classes. I loved learning about the computer. I knew there was good money in a career in this field. At the time, we were coding the computer using punch cards,

I just aged myself. I carried around stacks of cards used to get the computer to do what you wanted it to do. I was doing great, met nice people, and I even got a car out of the deal. Then it happened. I walked into accounting class, and the professor began to talk. I had no idea what he was talking about debit, credit, red, black. I was clueless. That was the last day I attended Alamance Community College (ACC) for computer programming. I quit. The voices in my head told me- *you will never comprehend the information.* I was convinced I was the only one in the class who was struggling. Once again, I made up an excuse. I told my parents I was getting a job; school was not for me. One of the reasons I stayed on my kids so hard about quitting anything they started was because I quit on so many things. I never allowed them to quit anything. Once they started, they had to finish. Have you ever walked out on your life because you were afraid? I did. It does not matter who you are; at some point, insecurity will rear its ugly head. It is up to you whether it controls you or not. Time and time again, I allowed my insecurities to control my life.

The effects of my limp would play out in my life on many occasions. I would dream only to have the dreams dashed by my limp. I realize now I am not the only one. Millions of people have died never seeing their dreams realized. Do not be one of them. Make the decision today to be an overcomer. I perceived my excuse for not going to college, when I was seventeen, as legitimate. And I am sure the reasons you give for not "doing" are too. I declared- "I will go to the community college, get a job, save money, and get an apartment.

And I did all of that. The excuses we tell ourselves for why we do not do, do not go, and do not perform, are just that, excuses. The problem is, we are lying to ourselves. The people around us accept our excuses as truth because they believe us because they don't know us. I became adept at hiding the fear and insecurities behind a smile and well-placed words. Brilliant, I wasn't fooling anyone, but myself. It is sad when you lie to yourself. The man in the mirror does not go anywhere. One day it will all catch up with you, and you will have to face yourself and acknowledge the lies. You can lie to me all day, and I may never know the truth. However, you can't continue to lie to yourself and expect to get away with it.

I realize now all the things I missed out on; the friends I never met, the relationship I never had, mostly the experiences I missed. Thankfully, God has a way of redeeming the time so that none is wasted. God uses every experience to shape us and mold us. One of my favorite scripture is *"All things work together for the good of the called according to His purpose."*[2] In the movie *Queen of Katwe,* a story about a young chess prodigy from Uganda, Africa, she had the talent and the know-how to beat any opponent, but she didn't always have the confidence. Her opponent wasn't the one sitting across the table from her. Her opponent was the voice inside of her that told her she didn't belong at the table. Because of the improverished town that she was from, and the living conditions she had experienced, this chess prodigy believed herself unfit to be in the same arena as the

---

[2] Romans 8:28 KJV

other players. In her final match to become a chess master, seated across from a worthy opponent, she allowed the voice in her head to take her focus, and she made a bad move. Her coach stood up and said, "You belong here." She won the match, and I am here to tell you, YOU BELONG HERE." My education was important to me; when my children were older, I decided to return to school. I was determined not to allow the enemy to rob me of this opportunity I received my Bachelor of Science in Christian Counseling from Liberty University, and my Master's in Biblical Education from Carolina Christian College. It is never too late to achieve your goals. God has a purpose for everything in your life the good, the bad, and even the delays.

You belong here. You belong at the table. Those are the words I longed to hear someone say. I waited years to hear them only to find out I was the one I needed to hear them from. I was waiting for others to give me permission to be great, and really all I needed was to believe in myself. Who are you waiting to get permission from: your parents, your husband, your friend, your boss, your boyfriend, who? They may never give you what you need, because it may not be in them to give it to you, and it may not be for them too. Everything you need is already inside of you, and until you tap into it, you will wonder this earth trying to figure out who you are. Your worth and value can't be defined by others. Only you and God can do that. God created you, and He created me on purpose, for a purpose. Don't let those voices in your head tell you differently. It took me a minute, but I get it now, I am "ME," beautiful, loving, trusting, creative, amazing, authentic ME. I am ready to face any obstacle and move forward, no longer impeded by a limp.

Revelation: It has a purpose. Keep moving. You are "YOU"

Chapter 3:
Limp of Fear

For God hath not given us the spirit of fear, but of power, and of love and of a sound mind. 2 Timothy 1:7 (KJV)

There will be a time, in all our lives, when we must face our fears. Fears of not being good enough, of being rejected, and fear of failure. That is when you will have to make a choice to rise above it or fall beneath it. It takes strength to stare down your enemy and come out victorious. There was a time in my life when I lacked the strength to overcome my limp. There is such a thing as healthy fear. It warns of danger and elicits a response flight or fight response. Reverential fear of the Lord is mandatory for our walk with God. It is a respect for His sovereignty and His Lordship. On the other hand, unhealthy fear is reacting to a perceived danger. There were many times in my life when I responded to situations, people, and things based on what I thought would happen. My insecurities fed my fear. I was always afraid of what might happen, who might reject me, or I may not succeed. Because of my fear of rejection, I allowed myself to be pushed into roles I wasn't meant to play. It was easier to acquiesce because refusing would mean rejection, so I smiled and went along with the program. It never occurred to me, *"what if I succeed"* at the time, it seemed easier to believe I would fail. I only had one view of my life. The glass was half empty, never half full. There came a time in my life when I realized I could no longer blame people. I had to turn the finger at me. I was the one holding me back. What has your fear cost you?

Revelation: 'For God hath not given us a spirit of fear, but of power, and of love, and of a sound mind." 1 Timothy 1:7

"I miss the train." That's the lie I told. I lied because I didn't want my friend to know the real reason, I was a no-show. I was afraid. Afraid to go to college and now afraid to get on the stupid train. I was invited by my best friend to visit for the weekend. She found the train schedule, and plans were made. I was so excited, and I was looking forward to seeing her and meeting her friends. I was to leave on a Friday, and she would meet me at the train station. I was still living with my parents at the time. My parents agreed and they were excited for me to go. So, what was the holdup? Friday came, and I was afraid to get on the train and I was equally afraid to call my friend to let her know of my fear. Instead, she waited for me at the train station with her friends. I just couldn't do it. She called me when the train arrived without me, wondering what happened. "I missed the train," I said. She asked the most obvious question of all, "Why didn't you call me?" I had no response. I don't know what my final excuse was. In hindsight, I am sure it was a lie. Why did I lie? Good question. If I told her the truth that I was scared she would be angry and think I was acting foolishly, so I lied. And the truth is I was acting foolishly. At that moment, my fear was more real to me than our friendship.

Here is the thing, when you allow your fears and insecurities to rule your life, you become adept at lying. You lie to everyone, even yourself, I did. I lied because I couldn't handle the rejection. I missed the whole point; she was my friend. She would have understood and would have suggested an alternative solution. I will never know. That ride could have changed my life. I never told her the truth. It seemed to be a moot point after she finished school. She moved back home. I was working full time, we got an apartment, and life went on. For me, though, our relationship was never the same after *the missed train*. And there were many times after that when I was presented with a plan, and I was too afraid to do it. One lie, one moment of surrender to fear, always led to another. For most of my life, I lived in fear of the repercussions of my choices, rejection, the stares, and the judgment most of my life. I did not go to college because of the fear of failure. What if I could not cut it? I would let my parents down, so it was easier not to try than to try and fail. What if something disastrous happened during the train ride? The failure was in the not trying. Stop living your life in fear. You will forfeit opportunities, and you will let yourself down. There is so much potential in us. That is why God made a point of reminding me of that over and over again. There is no reason to fear life, and all it may bring!

Revelation: Fear is meant to protect you, not to stop you.

Learn to recognize the difference. It will prevent you from relinquishing your power to something that is powerless. Stand up in your power! Let's go get it; get all that God has for us.

Chapter 4:
Limp's Impact on Motherhood

"Then Rizpah the daughter of Aiah took sackcloth, and spread it on a rock for herself, from the beginning of harvest until rain fell on them from the heavens; she didn't allow the birds of the air to come on the bodies by day or the wild animals by night." 2 Samuel 21:10

A parent's love is the first love the child learns to identify with. A love that has the power to shape the way the child views their relationships with people and with God. That is why our love for our children is so important and necessary. It gives them a view of unconditional love. It is my belief that a woman can shape and dictate the atmosphere in her home. And if the shaping is coming from a place of brokenness and heartache, that same love can distort the sound heard by her mate as well as her children. Even if we come from a dysfunctional home, we should strive to make our own home a place of wholeness. To do that, we must be whole ourselves. It is impossible to be sick or have any type of infirmity, and it does not affect those closest to you in one way or another. For better or for worse, my limp has had an impact on the lives of my children and my family.

There were many things I would have done differently. You've heard the saying, "hindsight is twenty-twenty." Now, I can when there were moments when I allowed my fears and insecurities to spill over onto my children. I had this fear what if what happened to me happened to them. Somehow, even in my failures, God was always faithful. He has proven to be a restorer. In my best effort, I couldn't prevent everything. My youngest was bullied most of his adolescent years. As parents, all we can do is our best and make every effort to teach them to love themselves and trust God with the rest. Like my parents before me, I did the absolute best I knew how to do, making mistakes along the way. To protect them from the "what if's" I made a decision that, in hindsight, should have never been made. I did well as a parent, except for some hiccups, my sons are intelligent, loving, gentle, and they love the Lord. They both have their own struggles, some of which come from decisions I made, BUT God. Please don't bash yourself for your parenting decisions. We have all made mistakes. Thankfully, God is always present to help us and to help our children. Some decisions were made out of lack of knowledge, not out of malice. There is a difference. Forgive yourself. You did the best you could with what you had. I pray my transparency will help someone else not to make the same mistakes I did.

When my youngest son was in middle school, he decided to stay after school to watch a basketball game. Granted, I didn't know he was staying. When I learned he didn't get off the bus, my anxiety went through the roof. I was expecting him to get off the bus with his brother, and when he didn't, and his brother called me looking for him, I panicked. When I learned his Dad had not spoken with him, that only exacerbated the situation. I drove to the school searching for him; when I pulled up to the school, he was coming out of the school with his friend. I approached him in a way that made me cringe when I thought about it; I yelled at him in front of everybody. It was awful. There is no excuse I can offer for my behavior, I was scared half out of my mind! Yet, I should have handled the situation with more grace and mercy. I thought my worst fear had come to pass; that he was hurt or assaulted, and I wouldn't find him. It takes a lot of faith to raise children because you can't be with them all the time, and they won't call when they should. It is important to remember that God is in control of everything. When it comes to bad decisions made by your children, take a deep breath before you respond. I had the tendency to react instead of responding, and we are all guilty of this. It takes maturity to respond to situations, and I was sorely lacking in that area at that time in my life. It was an over-reaction, to say the least. When it came to reacting to situations, I was either calm or exploding. There was no middle ground. I didn't know he was dealing with insecurities of his own. My rant did not help him at all. The situation could have been managed a lot differently. Now, even in my failures; I have learned to extend myself grace as well.

Revelation: It is okay. Learn from your failure, get back up, and start over.

I didn't know how to extend myself grace, I held myself to an unattainable standard, and that is why I was always failing to meet it. Give yourself some slack. It will make parenting so much easier. Learn to laugh at yourself, you will be okay, and your children will be okay. I wish someone would have given me that advice.

Revelation: Learn to laugh at yourself. It is the best medicine

"Because I said so" was my favorite response when I wanted them to do something or when I denied them the opportunity to do something. I never allowed them to voice their opinion. How would they ever learn that their opinion was important, and it mattered? In my effort to create boundaries, I was creating a prison, an impenetrable fortress, that I forced them to break out of one way or another. It took me a while to learn that. When my sons were a little older, they told me I never allowed them room to tell me anything because they were afraid I would get upset and yell at them. It is interesting, because the reason I never told anyone of the molestation, was my attempt to protect my mother and my family. Like my own sons, I was avoiding the fallout. Sometimes fallout is unavoidable and can be necessary to bring healing to the situation. In that moment of honest dialogue, I vowed to change my parenting approach with my sons and gave them the freedom to tell me when I was yelling or even being unreasonable. I don't know if they ever told me I was being unreasonable, but they sure told me when I was yelling. Nevertheless, it still broke my heart that my sons had felt that they did not have a voice. I wanted them to feel like they could tell me anything. I had created for my sons the same environment in which I was raised. The same perfection I demanded of myself, I demanded of my son. I never allowed them room for mistakes, or to experience life- because I was afraid they would get hurt. The perfection I wanted for myself and for them was a pipe dream. There are no perfect people, only a perfect God. From the outside, all people saw was the perfect mother and her perfect children. That's what I wanted them to see. We were far from perfect. Now I know that was a big mistake. Somewhere along the way, I forgot to be human and to allow them to be human. Being human means, I can enjoy my life with all its frailty and still serve God. When we put that kind of pressure on our children, they will eventually crumble under pressure, running to drugs, pornography, rebellion, and alcohol, all as a means of escape.

I am doing better, not perfect, better. Both my sons are grown, and I may not like or approve of their decisions; however, they are their decisions to make, and whatever the consequences, they are theirs to deal with. Parenting is hard and even harder when we put unrealistic expectations on ourselves and on our children. Then, we do more harm than good. We must leave room for our children to fail, even if it hurts. That is how they learn.

Chapter 5:
Limp of Insecurities

> "For you created my inmost being; you knit me together in my mother's womb. I praise you because I am fearfully and wonderfully made; your works are wonderful, I know that full well."
> Psalm139:13-14

Insecurity is a real threat to your dreams. Insecurity is one of the most effective tools the enemy can use against you, it will systematically tear down your belief that your dream is a possibility. You and I weren't created to think less of ourselves, because, in God's eye, you and I are beautiful. However, if you are led to believe you are not, then you begin to question your design, your purpose, and your dreams. We must remember that- you and I are *the apples of our Father's eyes*. (Deuteronomy 32:10)

Because I did not think I was beautiful, capable, or worthy of love, I worried more about what others thought about me than God's thoughts towards me. Even how I felt about myself, where I was going, and my dreams took a back seat to how everyone else felt. Would they like me? Would they accept me? I was more worried about how my decisions affected them and less about how they would impact my life. I should have considered God and myself above anyone else, but I never did. I lived my life never self-aware,

"I was looking to things outside myself for confirmation of my value, worth, talents, and abilities." I never thought I was smart enough, pretty enough, or good enough.

The good-looking guy in high school never asked me for a date, so I would try to force myself on him jokingly. It never worked. There was this one guy I really liked. He was a student-athlete, handsome, smart, and tall. He disrespected me on so many levels. I was measuring my self-worth and my value on whether he noticed me or not, whether he asked me out on a date. In my mind, if I showed up with him, wow, it would prove to everyone, I was okay. In all honesty, it would prove to *me* I was okay. No one else even cared! Always looking for someone else to affirm me. I would do anything to please people, lie, cheat and speak ill of people who had done me no wrong, all to fit in. What others saw and perceived as confidence was my failed attempt at fitting in. My distorted view led me to believe everything in my life wasn't good enough: my family, my car, my friends, and my house. In my "limp" filled mind, I felt perfect people were never rejected, shunned, or bullied, so I tried to be perfect with my imperfect self.

I thought God was like everybody else, so I tried to be perfect for Him, also. Whenever I failed to live up to my expectation of what He required, I would beat myself up. Sometimes it would take me days to recover, I would go into this dark hole, and I would have to dig myself out all because I thought I had failed God. It was the Word of God that got me out of the hole, yet I still struggled to believe the Word once I was out of the hole. It was really my unrealistic expectation of perfection that I was really trying to achieve. Throughout my life, I have always compared myself to others. They were prettier, smarter, and just all-around better. Their families were better, they had boyfriends, I didn't, the list goes on and on. Here is the big one, they preach better than me. From the beginning, I knew what God had spoken over my life, and I knew He anointed me to do it. I knew it. On some level, I just did not believe it. It was July 9, 2006, I preached my initial sermon. I was prepared mentally, physically, and spiritually. I had spent hours preparing with Pastor Larry Covington to make sure my calling was sure and that my sermon was contextually correct. Hundreds of people came out to hear what God was going to say. I preached a good word. I executed it well. I sat down, and it happened. That small voice, which seemed so loud, told me I had failed, I believed it, and I cried. My pastor was pleased, my family was pleased, and the audience applauded, and more importantly, God was pleased. However, the voice was all I could hear. The voice, which had been my constant companion contradicted God, and I didn't know how to handle it.

Revelation: "Submit yourselves therefore to God. Resist the devil, and he will flee from you." James 4:7

Just like in the past, I took every thought, every word as factual, and unfortunately, it cost me the joy of the experience. So many people believed in me, saw God in me, and it meant nothing because I didn't believe in myself. I would look at my acquaintances that I had assisted in their journey to finding their place in God and wanted to be them. In my eyes, their marriages were perfect, they were confident, and if the truth were told, they were struggling just as much as I was. I have spent my life wanting what someone else has, and in the process, breaking one of God's laws, *"You shall not covet your neighbor's house; you shall not covet your neighbor's wife or his male servant, or his female servant, or his ox, or his donkey, or anything that is your neighbors."* *(Exodus 20:17 KJV)* Tell that to someone else. I had coveting down to a science, and I did it time and time again.

My low self-esteem was a blight on my life, and it was intent on destroying any hope of me being who God called me to be. It was not until I got a hold of Psalm 139 and began to believe it that I realized God was never asking for perfection. He wanted me to be obedient, and the only way to be obedient is to believe every word He has spoken. We were created in God's image, that alone makes us perfect. What happened to you and even what you did to yourself does not define you. It is only a part of your story. The chapter may have been devastating. However, it is not the end of your story. You can change your ending and give God glory in the process.

Revelation: He gets the glory

Shortly after my mom died, I preached a sermon, "After the Chapter Ends," my text was Joshua: Chapter 1. Moses had died, and now God was looking to Joshua to lead his people into their promise. Moses had anointed and blessed Joshua for his new undertaking. Still, Joshua was afraid and looked at himself as being incapable of following in the shoes of such a great leader. What does that sound like? God, in His infinite wisdom, knew what Joshua needed to be successful. God encourages him to *"fear not and be of good courage as I was with Moses, so I will be with you."* God has made you and me the same promise. He is with us, providing us the strength, the courage, and the know-how to accomplish any task He has placed before us, so fear not. What made Joshua successful in his new role was not his ability. He was a great military leader. It was his faith in God. Joshua was one of the men who believed the Israelites were given divine ability to take the promised land, and he also had enough faith in God to declare it was time to cross over into their promise.

At every juncture in my life, God reminds me of that text of scripture. It has been my starting point, reminding me my past was the only building blocks used to get me to my next level. Though I haven't always exhibited it, faith is and has always been my key to success. The key to overcoming your insecurities is your faith and your obedience. If you believe God said it, and you believe He said it to you, then you can accomplish anything.

This is something I never could wrap my mind around. God never asked us to succeed. He asked us to trust Him and to obey His Word. Therefore, the outcome of my situation and my life is up to Him. And the same is true for you. God knows the things He has asked and purposed for our lives, which are beyond us to accomplish. That is where our faith should rise. Trusting Him enough to do it afraid, and in our weakness. Trusting Him enough to know He will not let us fall.

Revelation: He is bigger than what He assigned your hands to do. Trust Him with the OUTCOME.

Trust Him with the outcome of your life, ministry, marriage, and your children.

Chapter 6:
Limp's Effect on Relationships

"And if one prevails against him, two shall withstand him, and a threefold cord is not quickly broken. Ecclesiastes 4:12

"Iron sharpeneth iron; so a man sharpeneth the countenance of his friend." Proverbs 27:17

In preparation for this undertaking, I reread my journals. The more I read, the more I could see the challenges I faced when it came to relationships. Either I was trying to prove I was worth it, or I was being made to feel I wasn't worth the time or attention. Hindsight is 20/20, and there were times when I allowed my insecurities to override rational thinking, and I appeared to be desperate, always looking for a husband. Your limp opens you up for unnecessary disappointment.

Revelation: Every man and/or every woman you meet is not the one. Stop looking for what is not there.

My struggle for affirmation flowed right into every relationship, even into family relationships. I have never taken any relationship lightly. However, because I was struggling with who I was outside of a relationship, I struggled with who I was in one. Because of this, sometimes, I allowed my relationships to dictate who

I was. Self-awareness is vital to maintain mental and emotional health; it is imperative that you know who you are. When you are confident in who you are, you are less likely to accept just anyone and anything. You will require that your positive feelings and actions be reciprocated.

I brought so much baggage into every relationship, that it was difficult, or near impossible to create an enduring friendship or love connection. I agree with the statement- *people come into your life for a reason, season, or a lifetime.* I have many relationships that have endured the test of time, and truly, time is the measuring stick to evaluate any relationship. Those relationships which endured, have strengthened me and been an encouragement to me. I will forever cherish them. Despite my flaws, I found acceptance and love in those relationships. There have also been relationships that were only for a season. There are very few of my close childhood friends that I am in close contact with. However, I have one friend who has seen me through every event in life and has remained steadfast.

Relationships are 50/50. Each person in the relationship has a part to play in its breakdown, break up, or success. I am taking ownership only of the part that belongs to me. When a relationship ends for whatever reason, it is not a time to throw blame. It is a time to learn from it, go through the process of healing, and wait on God to move you to your next relationship. Many times, we get out of one relationship and go headlong into another without asking God for guidance and discernment. If truth be told, you probably entered the last relationship without seeking God's approval. I waited for God and then disobeyed God, there was a relationship I was in, and in hindsight, God had warned me in a dream, and I ignored the dream. I chose what *seemed* right versus what *was* right. And many of you can say the same!

Revelation: In order to avoid a repeat performance, seek God and WAIT PATIENTLY for Him to answer.

I waited, but never patiently. I needed the relationship to provide the affirmation I desperately needed. I waited 10 years to get into another relationship. If I had taken that time to find out from God what type of man, He wanted for me, my relationship would have been more successful. Instead, I spent my time bemoaning my situation and constantly saying, "I wasn't meant to be single, nobody wants me!" Pure foolishness, that's what it was.

Revelation: Your season of singleness is not to be endured. It is to be embraced and used as a time of preparation.

My limp has been a hindrance to opportunities and relationships. I sabotaged a relationship because, either I did not feel I deserved it, could handle it, or I needed too much from it. I required affirmation from my relationships. In hindsight, there were times when I wasn't the best friend to others. Someone once called me a "leech." I was offended at the time, but I must admit there were times, that is what I was. A leech latches on to its host and sucks the blood from the host, which weakens the host, but feeds the need of the leech. However, my insecurities and other flaws opened me up to be the "leech" in the life of others, and it has also allowed me to be leeched upon.

There was a time an acquaintance of mine made a false statement about a person I grew up with. This was my moment to tell them what they said wasn't true. I didn't. I agreed and even added my spin on things. Who does that? I was confronted about what I had said, and I lied. I was so concerned about being ostracized, left out of the in-crowd, and letting people down that I dishonored myself, and I let my friend down. I was that student who envied the popular kids but was never allowed in the group, not recognizing I was *already* in the group. When people weren't aware of my frailties, God was, and He hid me from total destruction. My need to please people has left me vulnerable to manipulation and abuse. I have allowed myself to be taken advantage of in the name of keeping the peace. Keeping the peace was my way of saying, "I don't want to be rejected, and neither do I want to fail."

Boundaries are necessary for any relationship. It is important they are set up at the beginning of the relationship. Six months to a year may be too late. You must know your negotiables and your non-negotiables. You must know who you are and what you want. The boundaries prevent you from compromising the standards you set.

Revelation: It is okay to be alone. It is okay to allow people to walk out of your life. It's okay.

There was an instance, when I was the aggressor in the relationship. A male friend and I became close, we talked all the time, he even accompanied me to my Christmas party at work. I really liked him, and we got along so well. We had our disagreements, but nothing to shake our friendship. Because he wasn't moving as fast as I would have liked, I got impatient, instead of allowing him to dictate the movement of the relationship, I asked him to move to the next level. Well, we know how that went. We stopped hanging out. I did not find out why, until later when he told me I had scared him. Fortunately, we are still good friends. How many relationships have you messed up because you wanted to be in control? I believed if I was in control of the situation, I could control the outcome. This was a fallacy.

John Bevere wrote a great book entitled, *"The Bait of Satan."* The book is about offense and how the devil uses it to get a reaction and to lead us down a rabbit hole. I remember the first time I read that book, and I could see myself, all in its pages. I spent my life being offended by one thing or another. In the aftermath of one of my failed relationships, I found everything the other person did, offensive to me. All this did, was keep me angry and frustrated. The goal of the offense is to create bitterness and resentment, both of which will put a huge wedge between you and God. I am aware of times when I was offended by something my partner said to me and would shut down in the middle of the conversation. I realize now, that was because I saw it as them telling me I was not good enough. It wasn't them that thought I wasn't good enough; it was what I thought about myself. My friend, being offended is a trap from the pit of Hell. Though my limp has affected my relationships, I have learned to walk in forgiveness, I have forgiven myself, and I have forgiven others. Do not allow bitterness and resentment to take root in your heart. You are better and worth more than that. Let it go. You will thank me later.

In a marriage, one should be able to see themselves in their spouse, a safe space to grow together. A good marriage demands maturity and commitment to successfully manage the ups-and-downs that come with two becoming one. I still believe in and endorse the sanctity of marriage; it is God-ordained. Marriage is a ministry; each party comes into the marriage with their own preconceived notion of what it should be and with baggage from their past. It is important that each party be mature enough to minister to the other, with patience, understanding, and forgiveness. Ministering may be the salve to promote healing for the wounds of the other. That is when true healing will take place. There are three things I learned from my failed relationships; marriage requires patience, marriage requires forgiveness, and marriage requires patience. You will get out of marriage what you put in. How much have you invested in your marriage? In your relationships?

Two marriages, two divorces unbelievable. I never thought I would be here. When I decided to marry, it was for better or for worse. I am forever grateful to my first husband because our marriage produced two wonderful children. We married young and were naïve, as my mom would say, "*still wet behind the ears.*" With this fantasy idea of what marriage should be and no real role models, we did the best we could. However, our inability to fight past our "limps" caused our marriage to break up, and our children suffered the consequences of our actions. I never wanted to end my marriage. It came to a point when divorce was unavoidable because of many things said and done. I cannot speak for him. However, I will say, "I was hurt by the things that unfolded in our relationship," as I am sure he was. When the desire to reconcile is not met with equal enthusiasm, it can make co-parenting difficult at times. Eventually, it got easier, and we settled into a routine. When it became clear that reconciliation was not an option, I filed for divorce. I needed closure and to move on with my life. Before we got married, we were friends first, and we have managed to remain friends. Maturity.

Revelation: Do not let outside forces (people) into your marriage. Other people do not get an opinion.

I was much older when I got married the second time. Still dreamy-eyed, I said, "I do." We started out well. However, we did not end well. Let God choose your mate, stop getting ahead of God expecting a great ending.

Revelation: Do not allow your marriage to define you. Allow it to refine you.

After my second divorce, I waited to change my name. My excuse was I earned it; I am keeping it. One day I was spending time with God, and I realized I waited because I was ashamed. What I had constantly failed to understand is the only one who has the right to define me is the manufacturer, and that is God. God created me and designed me in His image. I am God's masterpiece. You and I are perfect in God's eye. I had to stop being ashamed of what I had done, of what happened, and trust God for the rest.

Chapter 7:
Limp's Impact on Ministry

"For who makes you so superior? What do you have that you didn't receive? If, in fact, you did receive it, why do you boast as if you hadn't received it? 1 Corinthians 4:7

Comparison all but crippled my life and my ministry. I specialized in comparing myself to others. I can't remember a time in my life when I wasn't doing it, grade school, high school, job, marriage, always. I was a pretty good basketball player but was never consistent. In order to be consistent, I had to have a starting point, and that was knowing what type of player I wanted to be, and I struggled to know, so I drifted with every wind. My skill set would change with whomever I was comparing myself to at the time. I remember watching a college player, Len Bias, make this move when bringing the ball down the court. I tried to mimic it. My coach was furious and kept yelling at me to stop doing it. Learning from older, more experienced players is not a bad thing. The problem arises when it isn't working, and you keep doing it. The move worked for Len Bias, giving him clearance to the basket, so in my mind, it should have worked for me. This dysfunctional thinking only bled into my ministry because I never accepted who I was in the ministry, so I compared myself to others and tried to model my ministry according to theirs. As a result, I came away from each experience with a feeling of letdown and disappointment. When we compare ourselves to others, we agree with the plans of the enemy. It steals our joy and our truth. And I was declaring from the roof top I was not equipped for the task God had sat before me. By comparing myself to others I negated the truth of God's word, *"whom He calls He equips, and He qualifies."* Be alert that you do not get side-tracked by the lies of the enemy.

There were times I ministered, and I knew I was operating in the capacity God assigned me, and then there were other times I came away from the experience berating myself. I was berating myself because maybe I pronounced a word incorrectly, or maybe I didn't articulate the message as well as I wanted to. If you want to be successful and happy, don't compare yourself to others. Comparison is counter-productive; you look at the abilities of others and miss the abilities in yourself. Unfortunately, it is the easiest thing to do, especially when you have little or no confidence in yourself. There were moments of brilliance and power in my ministry; however, there were also moments of insecurity, indecisiveness, and a lack of faith. Not only did I struggle with a comparison problem, but I also struggled to believe God would do for me what He had done for so many others. I couldn't see beyond my insecurities to believe God for the impossible in my life; don't make the same mistake I did.

Revelation: God wants to do the impossible in your life and mine, to prove to you and to everyone, He is Lord of all.

When I started out in ministry, all I wanted to do was teach the Word of God. I had no intention of ever putting the word "Reverend" in front of my name. God had other plans. I knew as I know now, I wanted to help people, especially women, to find their way to freedom from bondage. I love teaching the Word of God, I have held classes for two to 300, and I never flinched at the number of faces because I loved what I was doing, and I knew I was called to do it. I knew God called me, but I struggled to believe beyond what I could see. I struggled in my faith and in ministry. If you are to complete your task, believing God can and that He will, is imperative. My weaknesses were exposed in my ministry, and the enemy was observant. The things I failed to do were not the devil's fault. They were my fault. I did it to myself. Have you ever gotten in your own way? I am the queen of it. God would say, "You can do this," and instead of replying in the affirmative, I would respond in the negative, defeating myself. God has a plan for our lives. Our job is to agree with Him, believe Him, and be obedient to Him. If we can do this, the sky is the limit. *Now Faith is the substance of things hoped for the evidence of things not seen.* It was impossible for me to believe God for the unseen when it came to my life because I never felt worthy of his attention. For years, my struggle was believing that despite who did what, God chose me, and He loves me. So, I had to stop fretting over my past, my failures and focus on the promises of God. Every word He spoke over my life will come to pass; my job is to believe.

Revelation: Your job is to believe that God can use you to do the impossible.

I even developed the terrible habit of pointing the finger of blame at others, for my failures and indecisiveness. Remember, I wanted to be perfect. It was easier to blame than to admit it was my fault. If you are teachable, God can use you. There were times when I could not manage constructive criticism. Instead of allowing the criticism to make me better, I saw it as labeling me as a failure. I now understand it was only to make me better. Thank God for growth. It is all part of the process. The difference between me and all the people I looked at as being successful, is they had faith in themselves, they embraced criticism, and believed in God's ability to work through them. They didn't allow unbelief to cripple their ministries. I was my own worst enemy, and I spent my life fighting against myself, instead of surrendering it all to God. I realized I put limitations on my ministry. All the times I stopped, all the times I doubted myself and God, I closed doors that were open to me. Fortunately, God did not give up on me, and He will not give up on you. God is going to complete your transformation. You must surrender to His method. He uses your whole life to mold you into the person He needs you to be. Relax, God has this!

Revelation: You decide success or failure. It begins with faith.

I mentioned in a previous chapter how disappointed I was in myself after I preached my initial sermon and the circumstances surrounding it. Your battle is not on the top of the mountain. It is when you come down. I didn't have enough love for myself to fight for myself or my ministry. I am so glad God has been fighting for me all along, even when I didn't know how far I was sinking. I am like Peter walking on water, thankfully I got close enough to Jesus that when I began to sink, all I had to do was cry out, and He reached down and grabbed my hand. You and the work God has assigned to your hands are worth saving. I loved pastoring, even though I think I could have done better. I made a lot of mistakes; some I wish I could get a do-over. I chalk them up to a learning experience. I love people. At this point in my life, I surrender my will to God. Day to day, I must remind myself to keep my focus on God and less on people. When I find myself slipping back into my old habits, I must do a quick mental check. This means sometimes, I must disconnect from social media; this helps me to maintain my peace. I have decided to do the work, to complete the process so that I can reach my full potential in God.

Revelation: Do the work; do not quit because it gets hard.

Chapter 8: Exodus

"and I have come down to rescue them from the power of the Egyptians and to bring them from that land to a good and spacious land, a land flowing with milk and honey." Exodus 3:8 (CSB)

September of 2020, I began to pack up my house, a house I had lived in for ten years. I had experienced love, heartache, and pain in this house. It was home. My reason for packing was still unknown to me, with no true direction. All I had was an unction, a knowing which I contribute to the Holy Spirit, and that was enough. I was coming off a seven-day fast, and I was in a different place in my life at this point. This was the first major step I had taken for God, and I was determined to trust Him. I started gathering boxes and getting rid of things. I did not tell anyone what I was doing. It was a stealth operation. Initially, I didn't know the purpose for packing; I just knew I had to do it. I packed the kitchen up first because that was the hardest to get done, and then I continued to travel throughout my home, packing up everything I didn't need. Because of the pandemic, it was easy to keep what I was doing a secret. I did not allow visitors in my home. The same was the protocol for the church where I was pastoring. I started cleaning out my office, getting rid of books, and things I wasn't using. It was important to make sure the paperwork for the office was in order. It made sense to keep silent about what I was doing because I really didn't know what God was doing. It wasn't that I thought anyone could talk me out of it. I did not want to defend my action because, to be honest, I didn't know how or why I was doing it. My decision and my actions were confirmed by people I trust with my life and through dreams. The dreams began early in the year. However, I didn't quite understand that the dreams were confirmation, until now.

In the midst of the pandemic, the church birth *A Heart of a Child Learning Academy*, which is a learning pod; a ministry providing a safe space for children to come and log onto their classes. We provided food and help with their classwork for eight to nine hours per day. The learning pod was up and running, with some hiccups, but running. I was excited about the new ministry and the direction the church was headed. So naturally, I was confused about the instruction I was receiving, but I kept packing up my things. Then in November of 2020, the same unction urged me to resign from the church as pastor. Now, I was really concerned, and I didn't immediately act on it. However, the feeling never went away. I was continually seeking God for clarification, I wanted to be sure it was not just me seeking release because ministry is hard, some days harder than others, and there was the added pressure of the pandemic. The following day I finally accepted what God was saying. I stopped by the deacon's house to inform him of my decision. He posed the questions I knew people would ask, "Why? Where are you going? Are you sure?" My answers remained the same throughout the process. "God is telling me to do it. I do not know where I am going or what I am to do. No, I am not sure, but I am doing it anyway." That following Sunday, I announced it to the church; they were stunned, to say the least. However, they graciously understood. When asked why I was resigning, my simple response was, "Because God said so," no further explanation was given or needed. By this time, I understood I had nothing else to give, I could not take them any further, and they deserved better. And 2020 was a hard year, and I was exhausted. By the end of 2020, I was no longer pastor at Awakening Outreach Church. Just like that, the life I had for eight years was no longer my life. What now?

After I announced my resignation from the church, my next instruction came, *resign from your job, pack up and move to South Carolina!* There were days of excitement and expectation, and still in the back of my mind was fear of the unknown. God was asking so much, so fast. This next step was the hardest of them all, my job provided my livelihood, and God was asking me to move and to move without a job. Wow! Moving into action, I finished out the year with the kids at A Heart of a Child Learning Academy. At the very end of that last day at the Academy, I emailed my resignation to my boss. I intentionally waited until the end of the day, because I was scared, and I was hoping my boss wouldn't see the email until over the weekend. That would give me time to get myself together. I hit send; immediately my phone rang! It was my boss. "What are you doing?"

I told him I was moving to South Carolina. "Do you have a job?" I answered, "No, I don't." His following response was, "Why are you resigning? Take the job with you." I was floored. If you trust God, He will surprise you every time, and boy, was I surprised! There was a time in my life when I thought He wouldn't do it for me, and here it was, God was doing for me just like He had done it for so many others.

Revelation: God is a Waymaker, a Promise Keeper.

I traveled to South Carolina to visit my son and began looking for a place to live. I gave God my must-have list. If I was going to do this, I wanted what I wanted: new construction, three bedrooms, and a garage. Would I have moved if I didn't get what I wanted? Yes, I would have, but I took Him at His word. I found a place with all my must-haves, but it was a purchase, not a rent. Though I make good money, I thought it was out of my price range because I had tried to purchase before and was declined. This is when we all say, "But God." I was immediately approved, and I was stunned! The process of purchasing the home took longer than I anticipated; it was my hope to be moved by the end of 2020. I did not end up moving until April 2021. Through it all, God was faithful. If you have ever purchased a home, it is the most gut-wrenching experience. There were days I saw progress, and then there were days when I felt I was taking one step forward and three steps backward. I continued throughout this process to write in my journal. A lot of times, we try to overt the *process,* either it is too long or too hard, and we give up. We miss out on our most important lessons when we refuse to surrender. Israel's refusal to endure the process cost them the promised land. Writing in my journal kept me committed to the process because along the way, I could see the hand of God. I had always heard- *God wouldn't ask you to do something without instruction*, and I sometimes wonder why I didn't get more in the details. Abraham, *"leave your family and go to a place I will show you,"* was a reminder of how God can request that which appears impossible.

In October of 2020, I saw a confession by an unknown author on someone's page on Facebook. I adopted it as my own.

*Help me to **PURSUE, OVERTAKE AND RECOVER** all according to Your will for my life. **NAVIGATE** me daily that my every thought, deed and prayer are intentional and that my follow-through is equally precise!*

*Let me **NOT** be easily persuaded by things, people, and positions of this world. **BUT** instead, assist towards change. Lord God, I give myself away that you can use me.*

Because I wanted to change the way I was operating, I read it every day before leaving my house. I wanted to walk differently and to believe differently. I wanted to change my life. I wanted to know what it was like to walk by faith.

Some My Journal Entries:

11/24/2020: In a dream, I was given an evergreen bush, the kind that covers the ground(spreads).

Me: I am going to plant it so it can spread
God: That is good
Me: Where shall I plant it
God: South Carolina

11/25/2020: The thought of resigning from my job terrifies me. How will I survive, pay my bills, eat, and keep a roof over my head? Let alone relocate with $1000 in the bank. I do not think I can do this.

12/30/2020: I want to finish this year differently than inyears past. I want to finish in faith, trusting God for the impossible. There is so much God wants to do for me. It is time to walk on water!!!

1/4/2021: I compare this time in my life to that moment when you are between hairstyles. Your hair is too short for the design you want and too long for the one you had. At this moment, I am in between where I was and where I am going. No church to call home, no pulpit to preach from, no church family. I am lost without it all. Do I get frustrated and go back, or do I push forward to see what God has for me? To make sure there was no going back, Elijah destroyed everything to go with Elisha. 1King 19: 21

1/5/2021: One day, I am filled with confidence, excitement, and the next, concern and doubt. I have reminded myself of God's plans and purpose to override the negative feelings. I am glad the pages of our lives change. God: Turn the page

1/8/2021: I CAN'T ------------- HE CAN --------SO ------------- I WILL -I realize I am dependent on God. *Dependence is "a state of relying on our being controlled by someone or something else"*

I moved in, still pinching myself because I was really in my home, a home God gave me. A fresh start is what He gave me. I would sit in my house, sometimes trying to wrap my mind around what God had done for me; I marveled at His faithfulness. I was overwhelmed with gratitude. One month into my move, I injured my leg. I am not sure when it happened or what happened. On a scale of one to ten, the pain in my leg was a 15! I could not climb the steps in my house; I had to sit down and pull myself up, one step at a time, and I crawled from room to room. It even hurt for the bed cover to touch my leg. I can best describe it as my nerve endings in my legs were standing on end, and any touch sent a sharp pain shooting through my leg into my knee. After two visits to the emergency room, pain medication, muscle relaxers, Advil, Tylenol, and a lot of tears, all I learned was it was either the sciatica nerve or an injured iliotibial band (ITB). Limited by my mobility, I was confined to my house. My bed and couch became my friend, I had groceries delivered. I tried once to go to the grocery store, and I thought I would die. The pain was so bad. My trainer from back home gave me exercises to do. I began doing those, and eventually, the pain lessened. I finally was able to make a trip home to see my father. The entire visit, I had to sit with my leg propped up. It did not matter; I was with my family and no longer isolated.

Genesis 32:25 When the man saw that he could not defeat him, he struck Jacob's hip socket as they wrestled and dislocated his hip.

When I read that scripture, I felt the same unction that brought me to South Carolina. Y*ou have been limping through life.* You have allowed your movement, your progression, your relationships, your ministry, and your life to be limited by your past. It was as if a light bulb went off in my head, and I knew at that moment I had done just that. I had allowed the enemy to use every wound, every heartache, and disappointment as a weapon against me and my dreams. The dreams God had given me were mine to fulfill, and more importantly, I wasn't what the devil made me believe I was. I am not weak, ugly, less than, or someone to be mistreated, misused, or abandoned. Confirmation came on a journey home in the parking lot of Food Lion. A dear friend of mine and I were talking, and I was telling her about my injury and the struggle I had recovering. In the middle of the conversation, she said, "You were limping through life, and now you are no longer limping. God has healed you." And that is exactly what He did, God healed me. Not only did He heal me, but He also freed me.

Revelation: The healing process can be more painful than the wound. Brace yourself.

Just as the healing for my leg was a process, my freedom from all the mess in my life is a process, and this book is the vehicle God is using. A limp impedes forward progression. It doesn't stop it, but it does slow it down. Often in my life, I have allowed my limp to not just slow me down, but literally stop me. I blamed everyone else, and my leg injury reminded me if you want out of any situation, you must put the work in. Don't allow the events of your life to hinder you. God has placed dreams in each of us. Yours have yet to be realized. I do not know what your limp is. The thing that keeps you denying who you really are, can be overcome. Spending time with God is required for you to move on. I sometimes think my move was all about isolation; isolating me away from the busy life I was living. I was busy, but sometimes I wasn't very productive. This move gives me the opportunity to reflect and start over.

Revelation: It is okay to start over.

Sometimes the process of freedom can seem harder than staying bound. My recovery from my injury was sometimes more painful than sitting on the floor, but if I wanted my mobility back, I had to go through it. One morning I was walking the dog, and she started to run. Under normal circumstances, I would have run along with her, but this morning she started running, and I fell. My leg just gave out. It was that morning I decided this wouldn't happen again. I endured the pain of exercise and the nights of soaking in the tub to ensure that my knee would be strong enough to carry my weight. Your freedom will come at the expense of some tears, some anger, forgiveness, and a whole lot of prayer. You are worth it. Your dreams are worth it. That is what happened with my ministry. I had lost power and strength because I was so focused on ministry that I didn't take the time I needed to spend with God. This move has afforded me the opportunity to spend more quiet time with God, not preparing to preach, just to hear what He is saying to me. I have had to face some hard truths about myself. God has been gentle in His chastisement. I am grateful. God has been faithful through this process. He has encouraged and reassured me that even this is necessary for my healing. There have been days while writing that I wondered who would read it and who even cares about my limp. God reminds me every time, **"It isn't for them. It is for you."** I know it is for you, too, mostly it is for His Glory.

Submit your will to God. It is truly *"His will, not your will,"* if you want to walk in true victory. That is exactly what I had to do. I had to surrender because I had been declaring to the world I was walking in victory, and in some areas of my life, I was walking in defeat. I had begun to believe I had gotten all I deserved, because of my failure. God desires more for us. The man at the gate called *Beautiful*, had gotten comfortable lying at the gate. Peter and John were there to remind him he deserved to go through the gate. God reminded me of the many things that I deserve, not because of who I am but because of who He is. God says I deserve to stand before thousands, to have a seat at the table, to be loved, and to be cherished. Now, I am reminding you that you are worth it! You too, deserve to have your dreams fulfilled. Go through the process no matter how hard it gets. There will be days when you think you can't take much more, remember God loves you and wants you to be healed and free.

But Jesus turned him about, and when he saw her, he said, Daughter, be of good comfort, thy faith hath made thee whole. And the woman was made whole from that hour. Matthew 9:22

YOU GOT THIS!!!!

References

Nelson's Super Value Series (Book)- Nashville: Thomas Nelson Publisher, 1986.
What's Really Holding You Back? (Book)/Auth. Burton Valorie- Colorado Springs: Waterbook Press, 1982.

ABOUT THE AUTHOR

Amy **TIMMONS**

Amy Timmons

Rev. Amy Timmons was born and raised in Burlington, North Carolina. She is the youngest daughter to Henry Timmons Jr. and the late Gloria P Timmons. She has two sons, Joseph and Joshua. She has two beautiful grandbabies, Lauryn and Kamryn. She received her B.A. degree in Religion and Christian Counseling from Liberty University. She also received her Master of Religious Education from Carolina Christian College.

Amy preached her initial sermon, July 9, 2006. Rev. Timmons served as an Associate Minister at Ebenezer United Church of Christ under the leadership of Rev. Dr. Larry Covington. Under his leadership, she facilitated many small group studies as well as taught Christian Education Classes. She has been a strong supporter of women and youth ministries.

Rev. Timmons performed many duties, under the leadership of Rev. Dr. George Pass Sr. at St Matthews AME Church in Burlington. She has organized and led conferences, directed and provided women a place of freedom, worship, study, and growth.

Rev. Timmons was the Senior Pastor at Awakening Outreach Church Inc. formally Immanuel Christian Center, Inc in Burlington, NC. She is the founder of Pursuing Wholeness Ministries; ministry devoted to encouraging, maturing, and the healing of God's people. Rev. Timmons is the visionary behind, A Heart of a Child Learning Academy, a learning pod for elementary age children during the pandemic. Providing them a safe place to continue to learn and grow. Because of her love for God and for His people she has promised to devote her time, gifts and resources to the kingdom of God.

Rev. Timmons is employed as an Commercial Accounts Manager with Piedmont Triad Insurance Agency. In her spare time, she likes to focus on her many hobbies; reading, movies, spending quality time with family and friends.

Rev. Timmons strives to influence the people of God by encouraging and inspiring them in their walk with Christ. Amy is in awe of the patience of God, realizing in her best effort, she sometimes falls short. She is often reminded of the faithfulness of God. Her favorite scripture is Philippians 1:6: ***"Being confident of this very thing, that he which hath begun a good work in you will perform it until the day of Jesus Christ".***

The HIDDEN Limp

Amy Timmons

Amy Timmons

THANK YOU FOR YOUR SUPPORT

shero
publishing

Made in the USA
Columbia, SC
13 November 2021